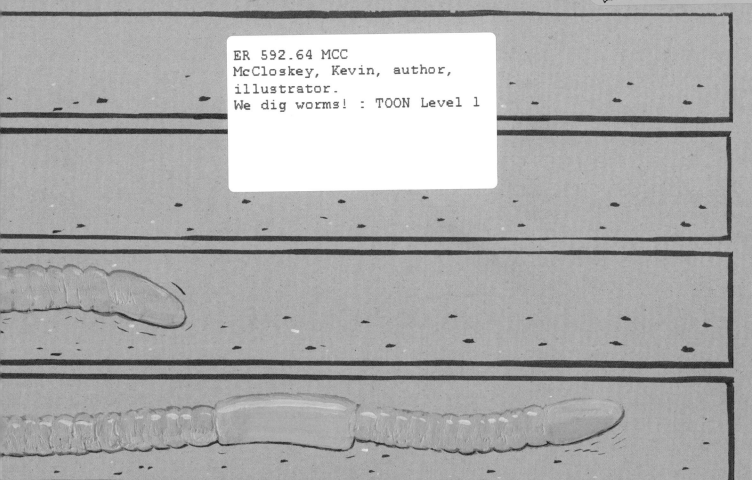

For my wife, Mama Patt,
who asked for a fun worm book to read at the library.

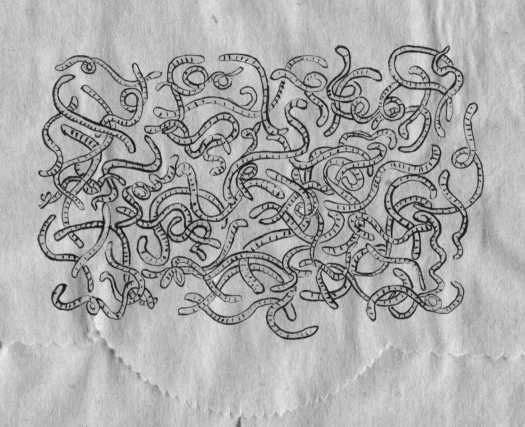

WE DIG WORMS!

A TOON BOOK BY

KEVIN McCLOSKEY

1/6 DUROTUFF

DURO BAG MFG. CO.

Elizabeth, NJ 07201

Made in USA

ERNESTO CRUZ

EL 05 A

Editorial Director: FRANÇOISE MOULY

Book Design: FRANÇOISE MOULY

Deputy Editor & Production: SASHA STEINBERG

KEVIN McCLOSKEY'S artwork was painted with acrylics and gouache on recycled paper bags.

A TOON BOOK

 All our books are Smyth Sewn (the highest library-quality binding available) and printed wiht soy-based inks on on acid-free, woodfree paper harvested from responsible sources. Printed in Shenzhen, China by Imago. Distributed to the trade by Consortium Book Sales; orders (800) 283-3572; orderentry@perseusbooks.com; www.cbsd.com.

Library of Congress Cataloging-in-Publication Data: McCloskey, Kevin, author, illustrator. We dig worms! : TOON Level 1 / by Kevin McCloskey. pages cm

Summary: "Young children (and a hungry bluebird) follow a talkative earthworm around. They learn fun facts about worms and their important role in our environment."--Provided by publisher. ISBN 978-1-935179-80-1 1. Earthworms--Juvenile literature. I. Title. QL391.A6M325 2015 592.64--dc23 2014028775

ISBN 978-1-935179-80-1 (hardcover)

15 16 17 18 19 20 IMG 10 9 8 7 6 5 4 3 2 1

www.TOON-BOOKS.com

THERE ARE MANY DIFFERENT WORMS.

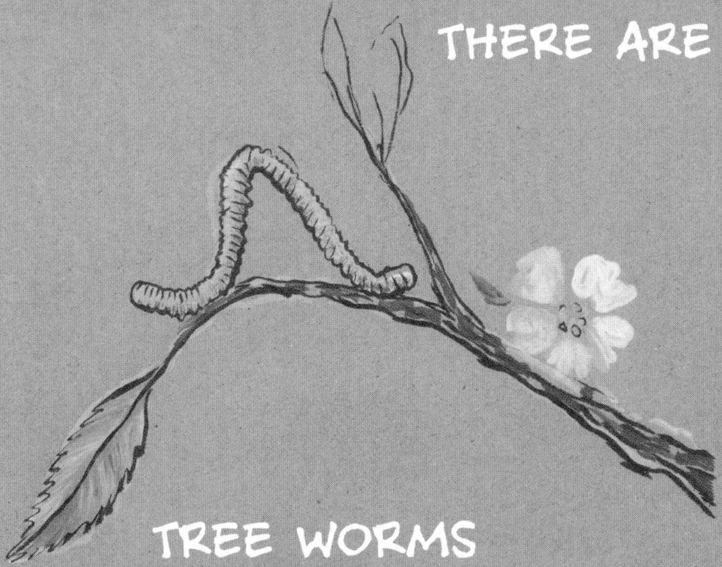

TREE WORMS

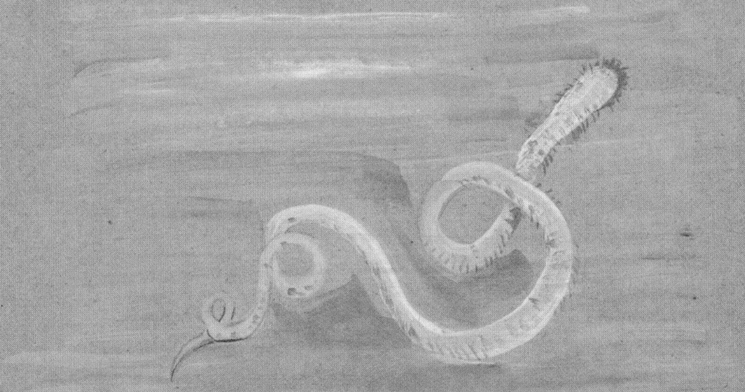

SEA WORMS

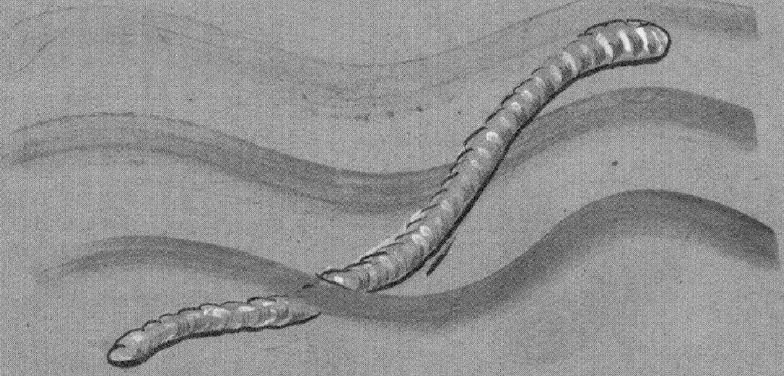

RIVER WORMS

...AND GUMMMY WORMS!

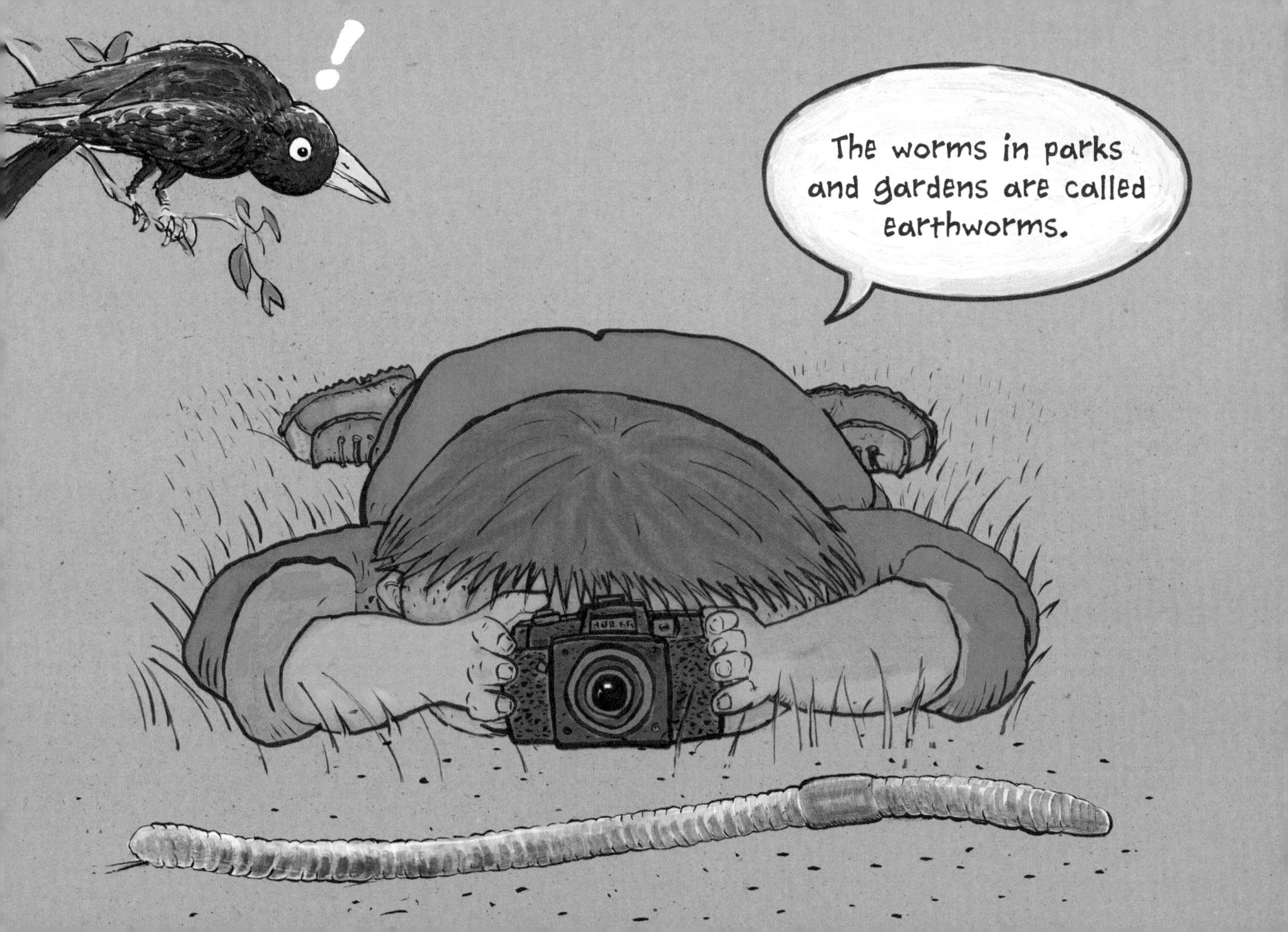
!
The worms in parks and gardens are called earthworms.

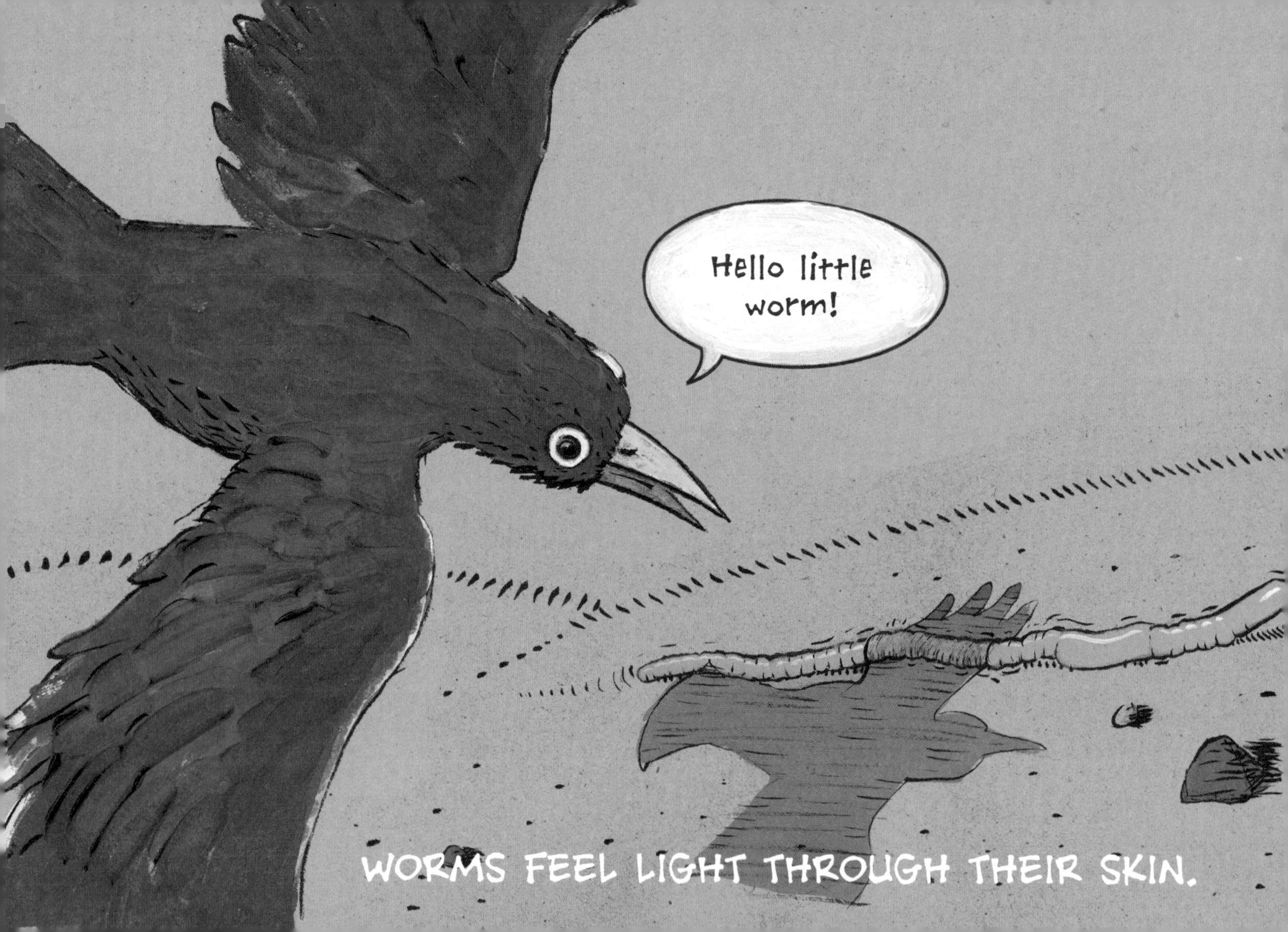
Hello little worm!
WORMS FEEL LIGHT THROUGH THEIR SKIN.

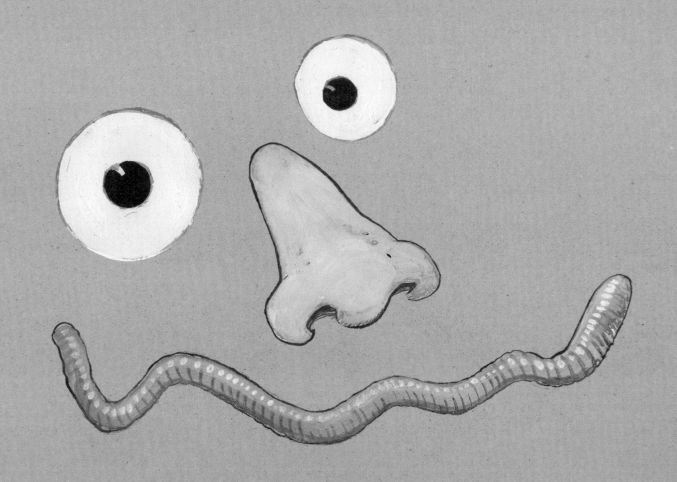

THEY HAVE NO **EYES** AND NO **NOSE.**

WORMS DO A LOT OF IMPORTANT WORK.

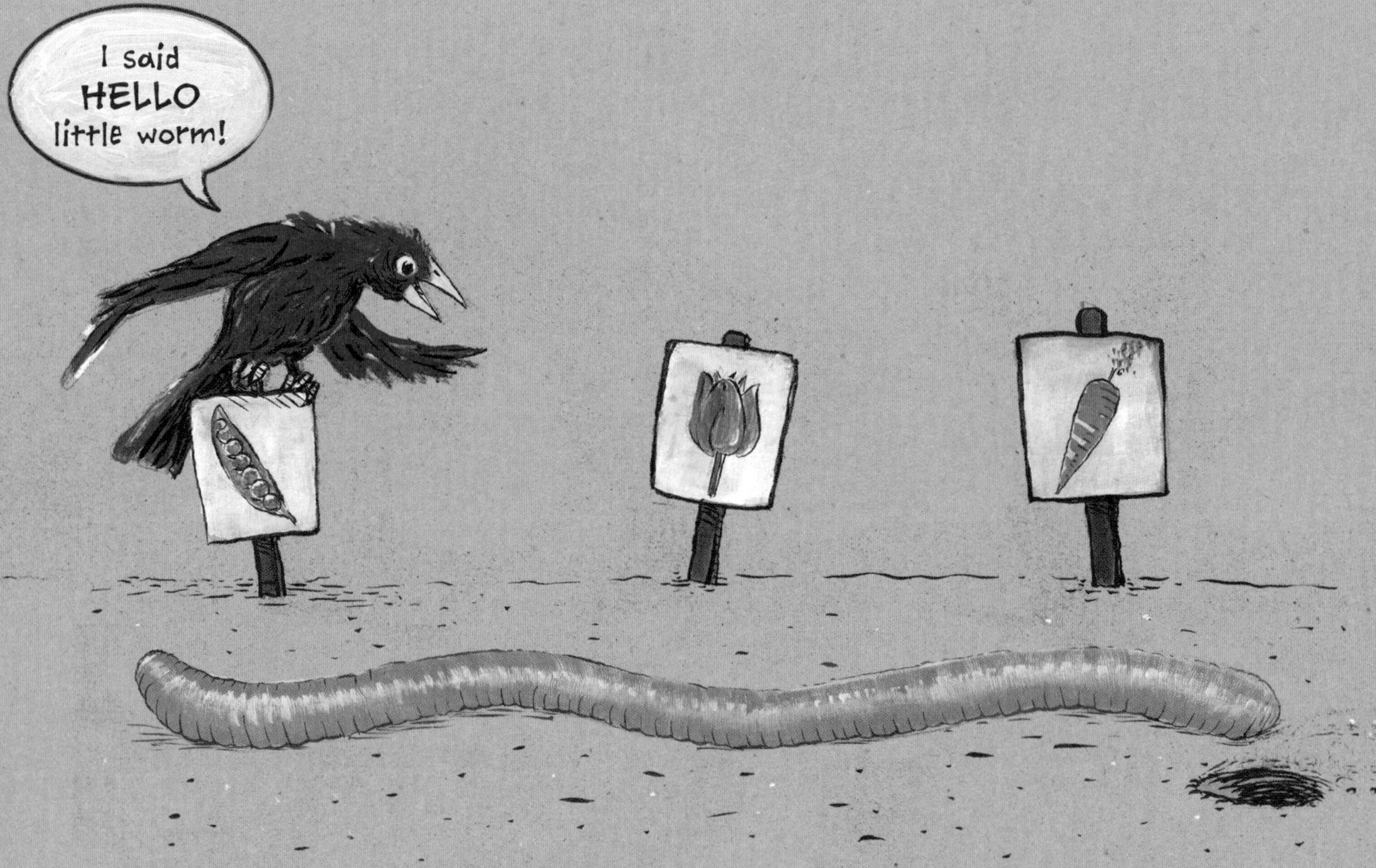
I said HELLO little worm!

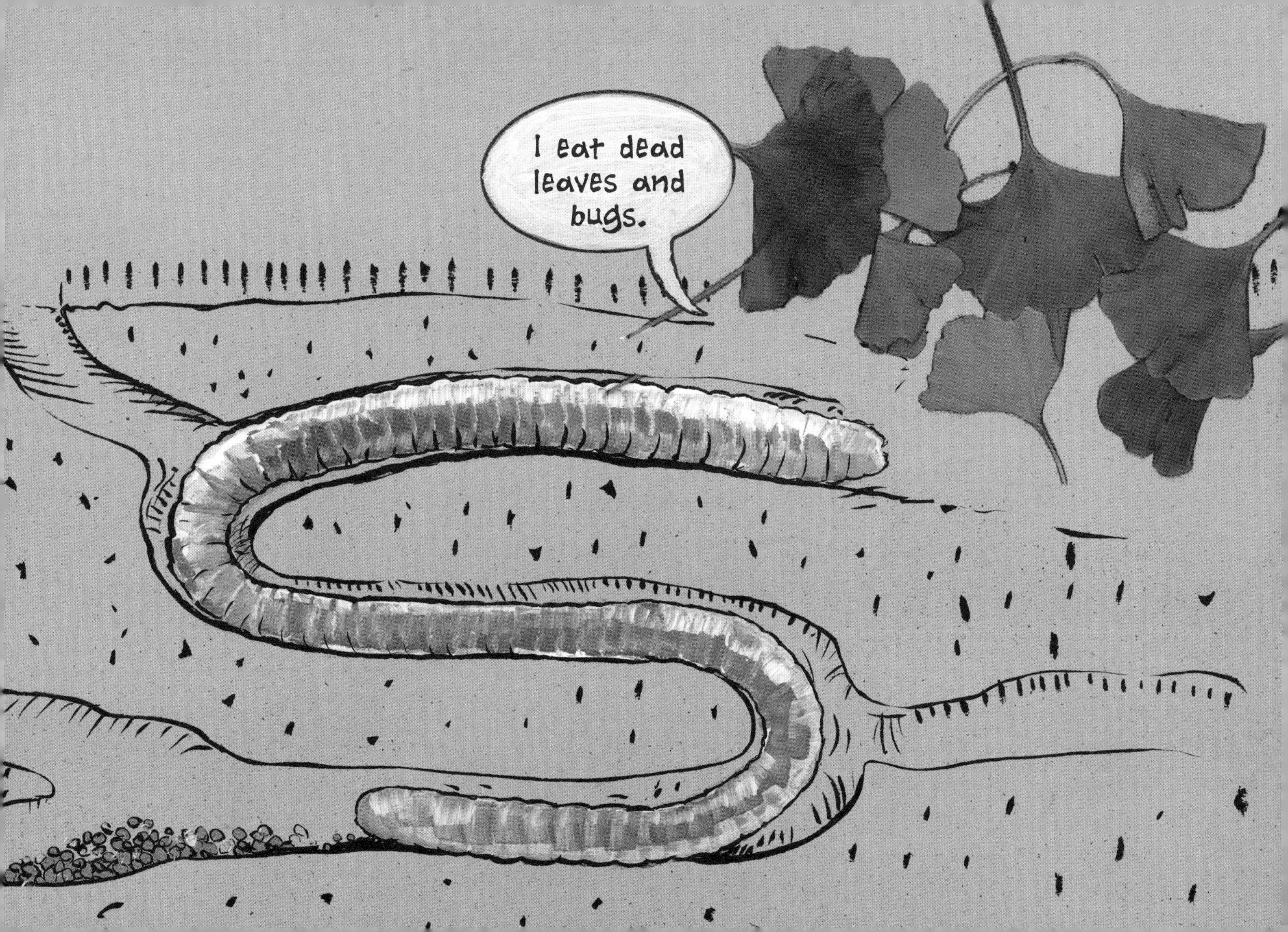
I eat dead leaves and bugs.

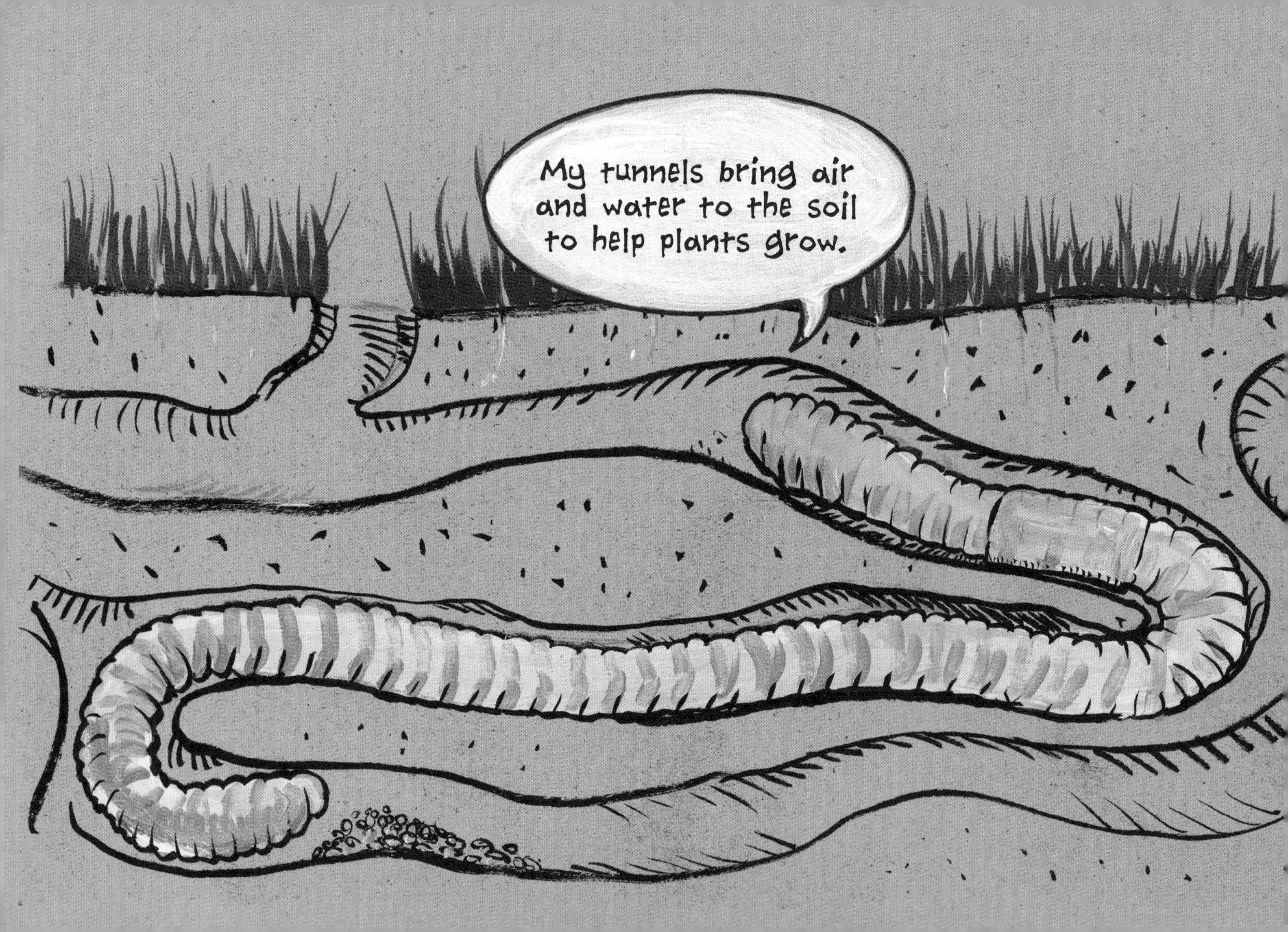
My tunnels bring air and water to the soil to help plants grow.

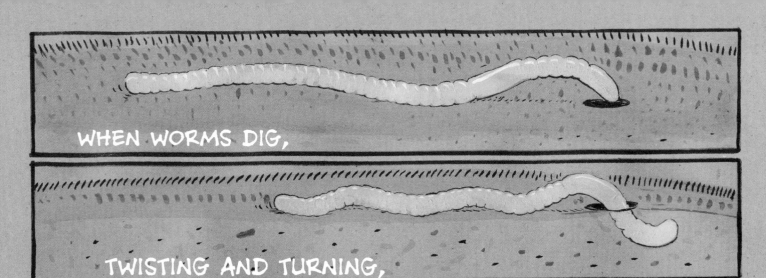

WHEN WORMS DIG,

TWISTING AND TURNING,

THEY MAKE THE EARTH...

...EARTHIER.

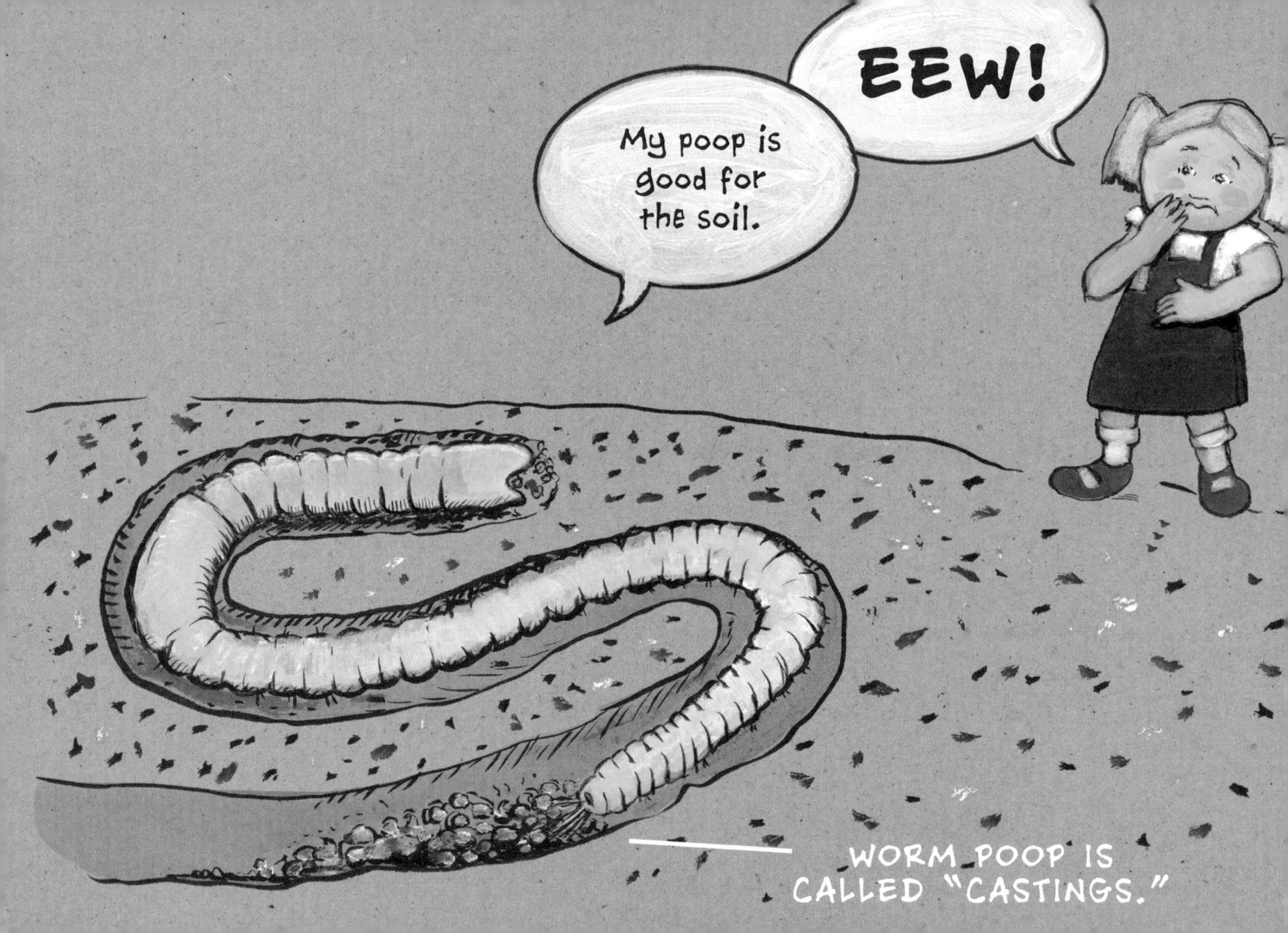
My poop is good for the soil.
EEW!
WORM POOP IS CALLED "CASTINGS."

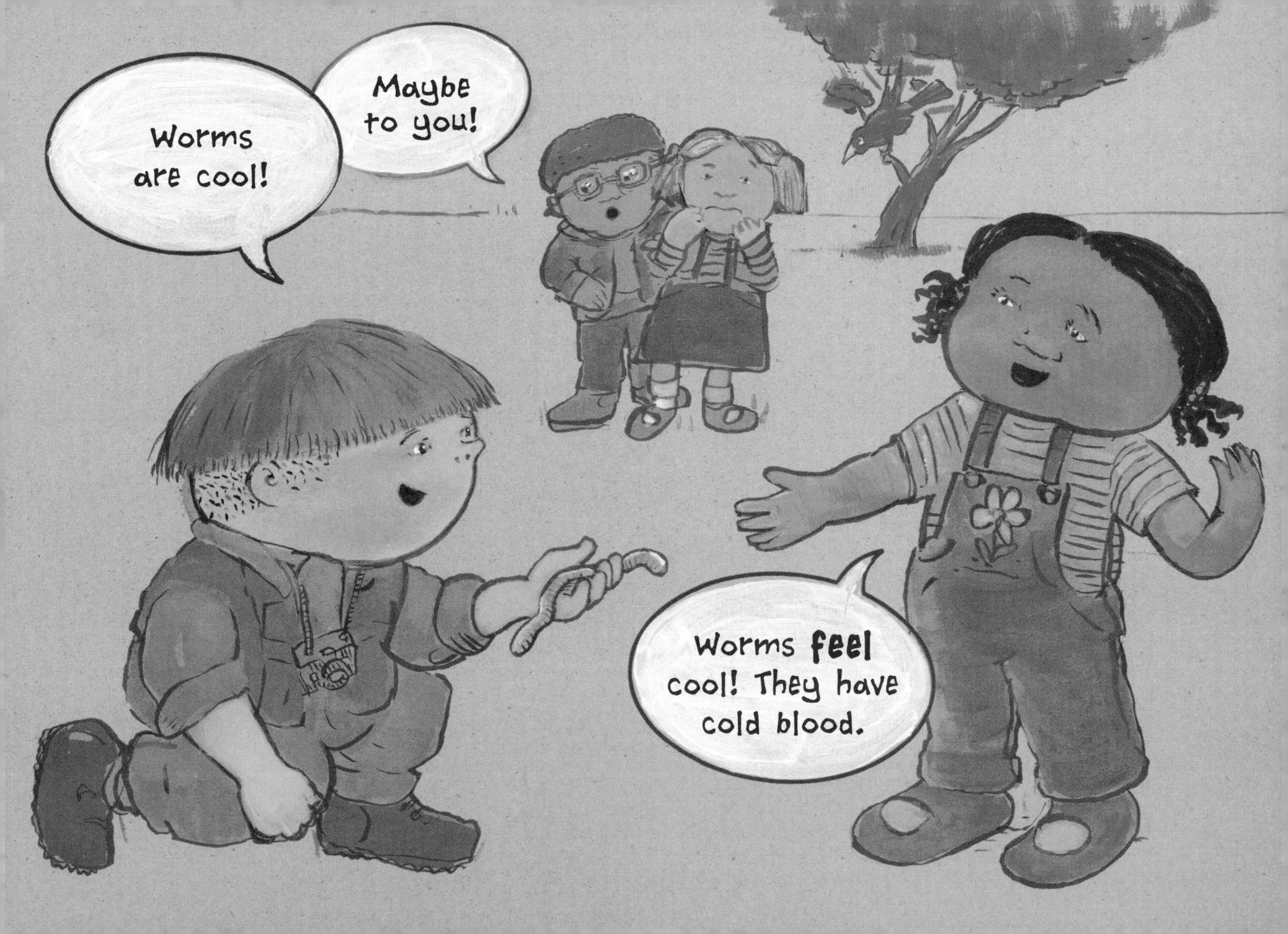
Worms are cool!
Maybe to you!
Worms **feel** cool! They have cold blood.

COCOONS

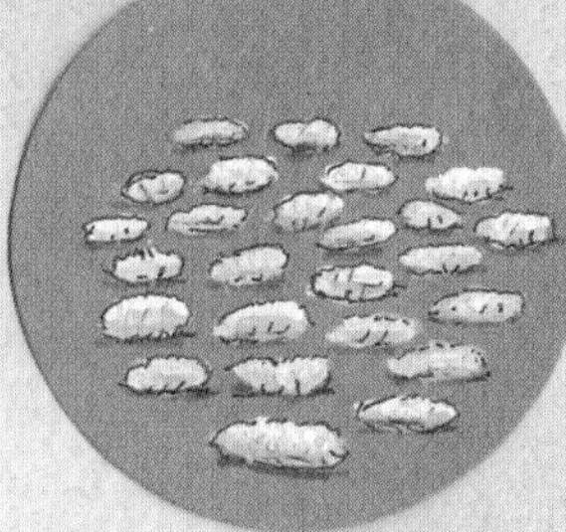

Worms are born from cocoons.

SETAE

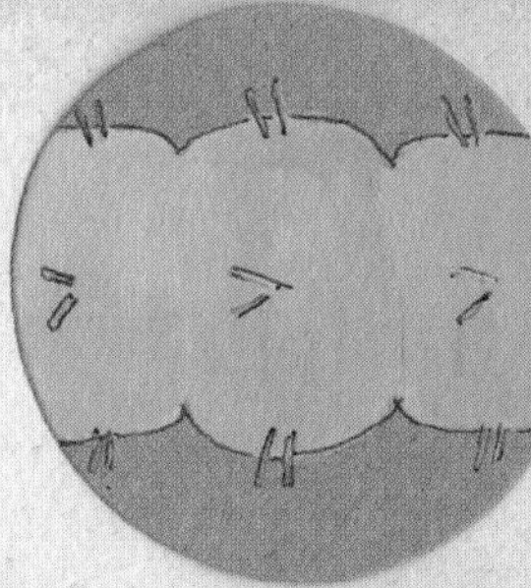

Setae are tiny bristles that help worms move.

OUTSIDE:

Worms don't have lungs. They breathe through their skin.

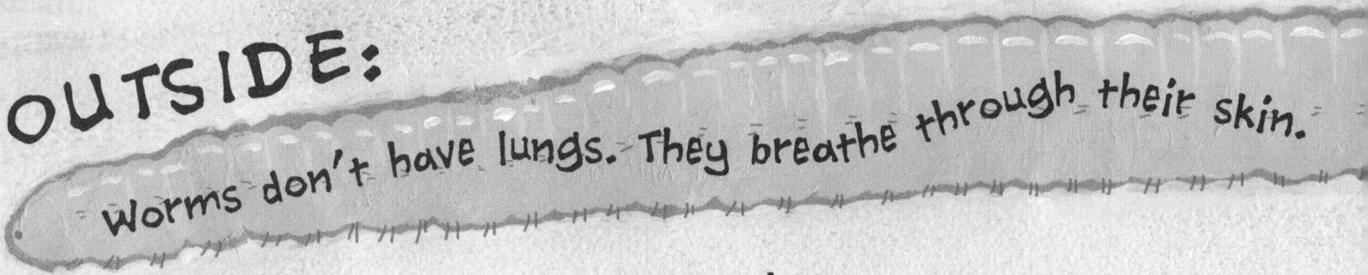

INSIDE:

Only muscles & nerves. Worms have no bones.

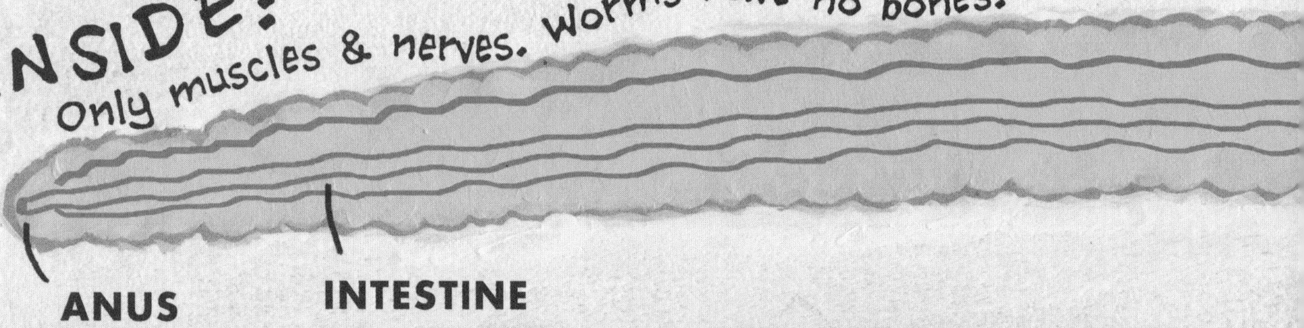
ANUS
INTESTINE

MAP OF THE WORM

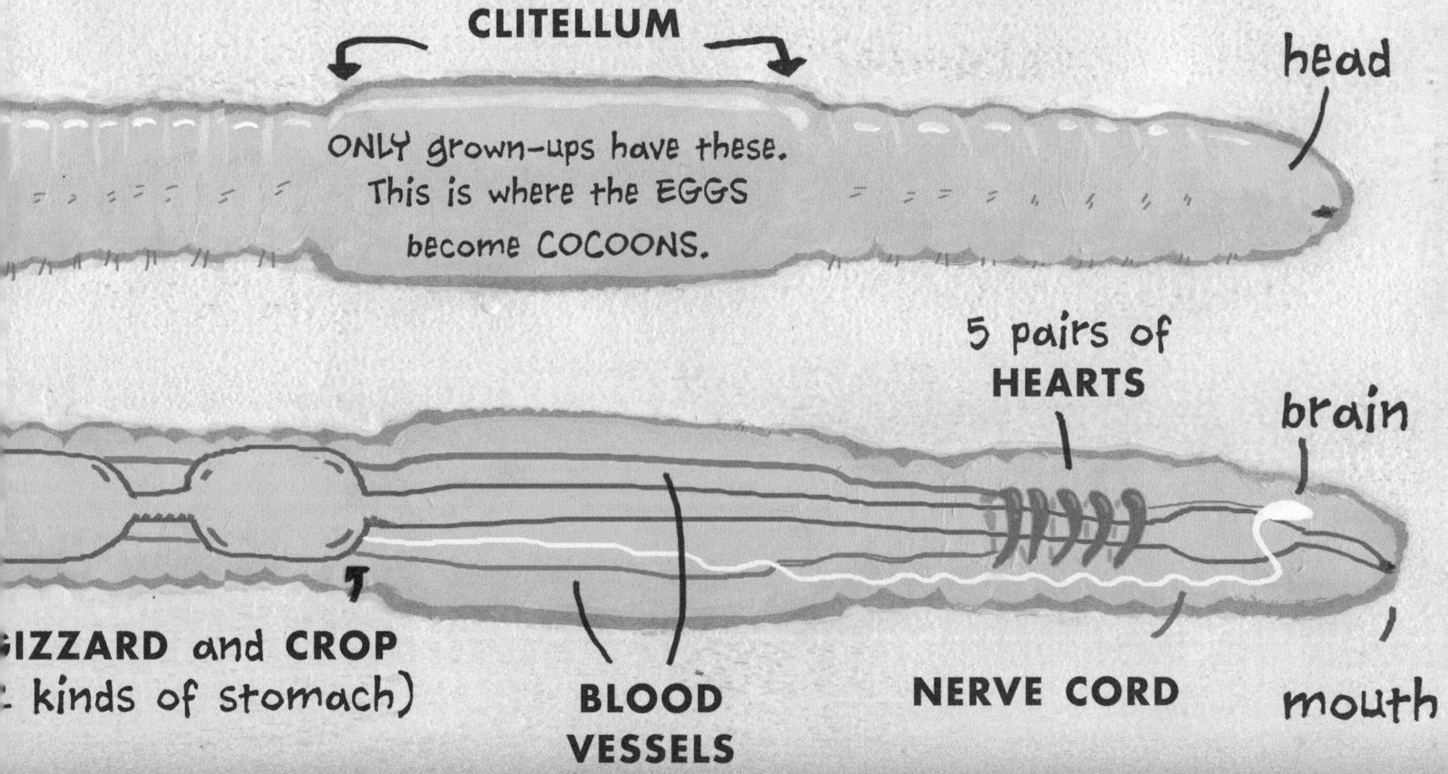
CLITELLUM
head
ONLY grown-ups have these.
This is where the EGGS
become COCOONS.
5 pairs of
HEARTS
brain
IZZARD and CROP
kinds of stomach)
BLOOD
VESSELS
NERVE CORD
mouth

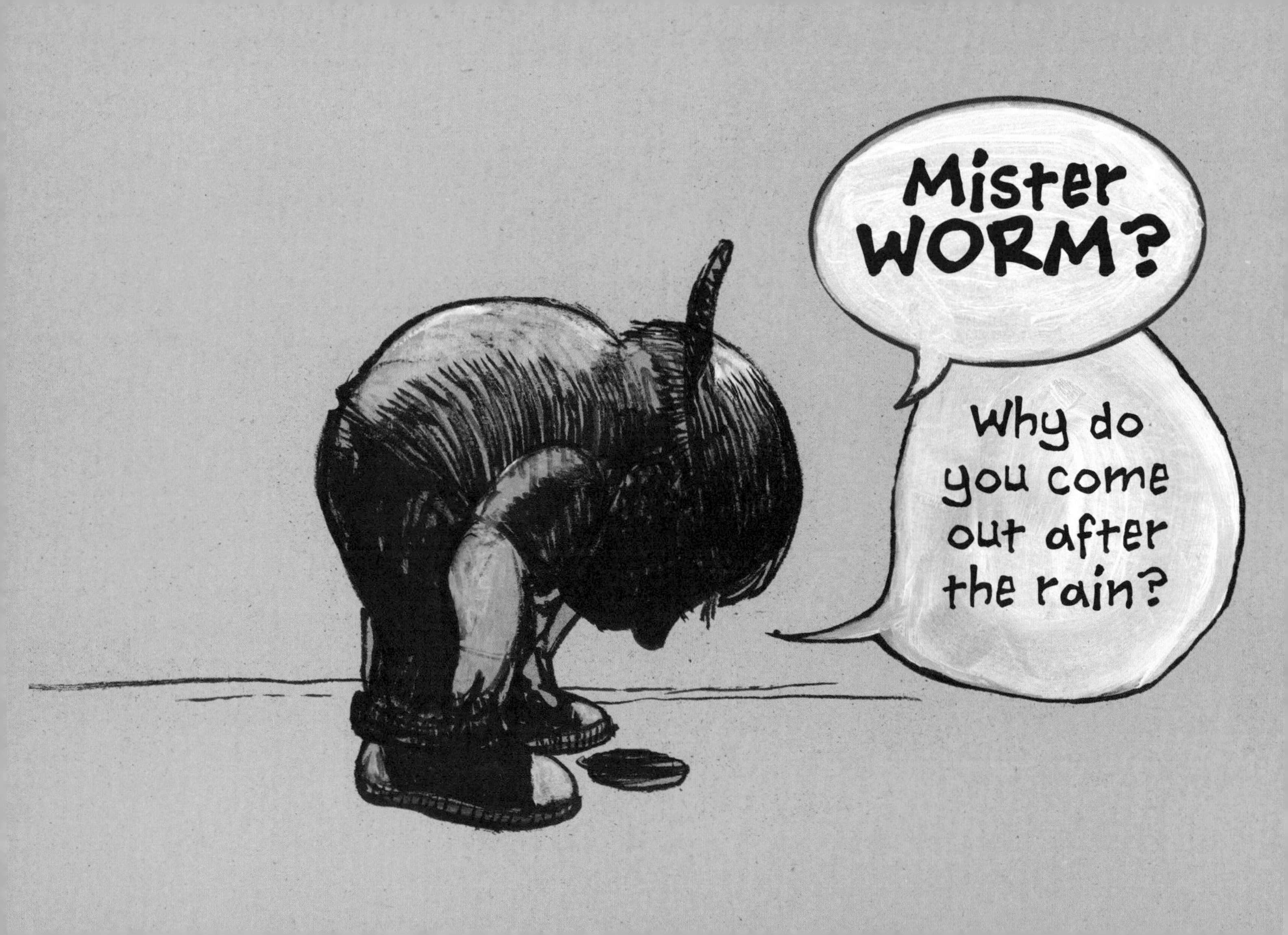
Mister WORM?
Why do you come out after the rain?

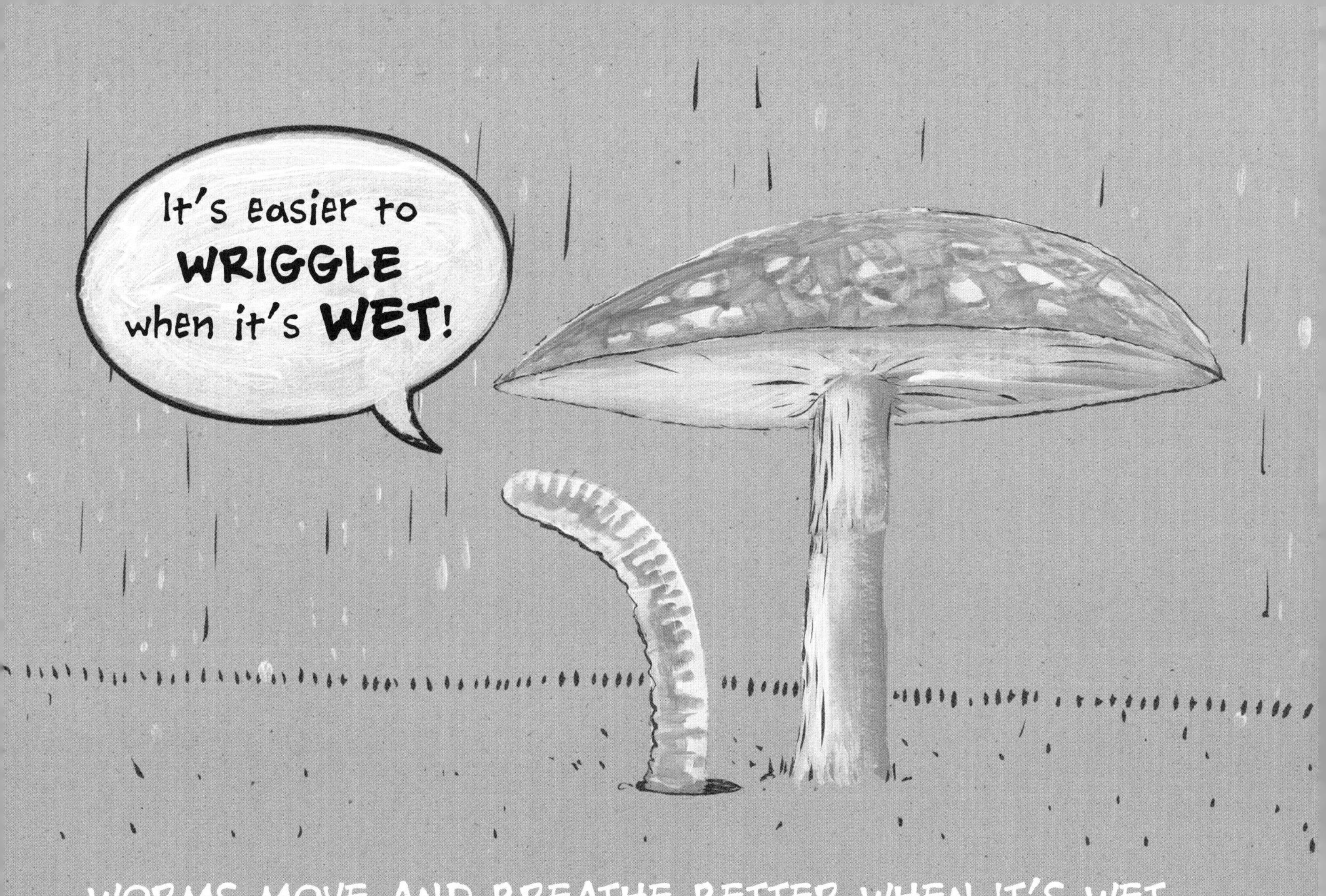
It's easier to WRIGGLE when it's WET!

WORMS MOVE AND BREATHE BETTER WHEN IT'S WET.

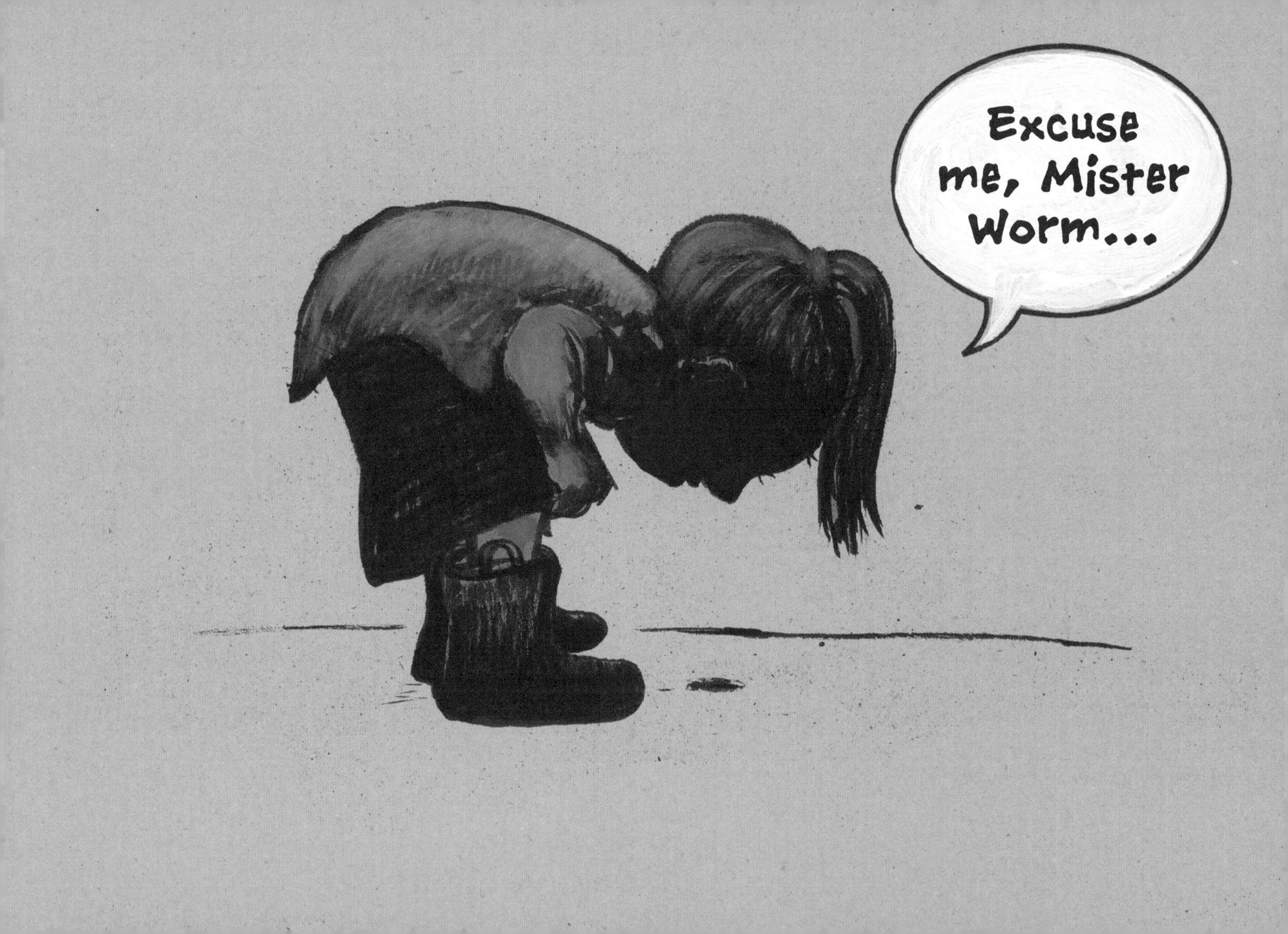
Excuse me, Mister Worm...

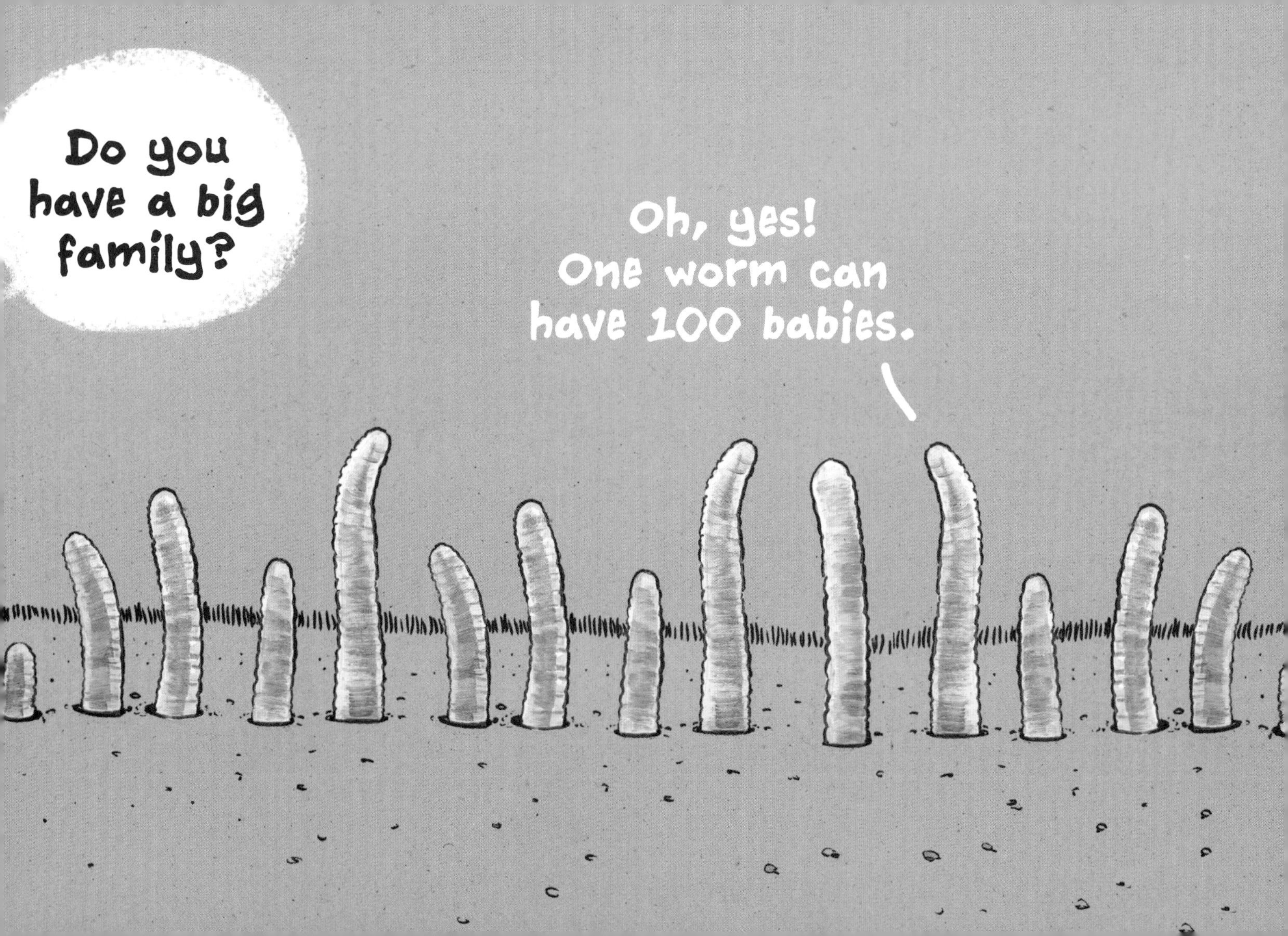
Do you have a big family?
Oh, yes! One worm can have 100 babies.

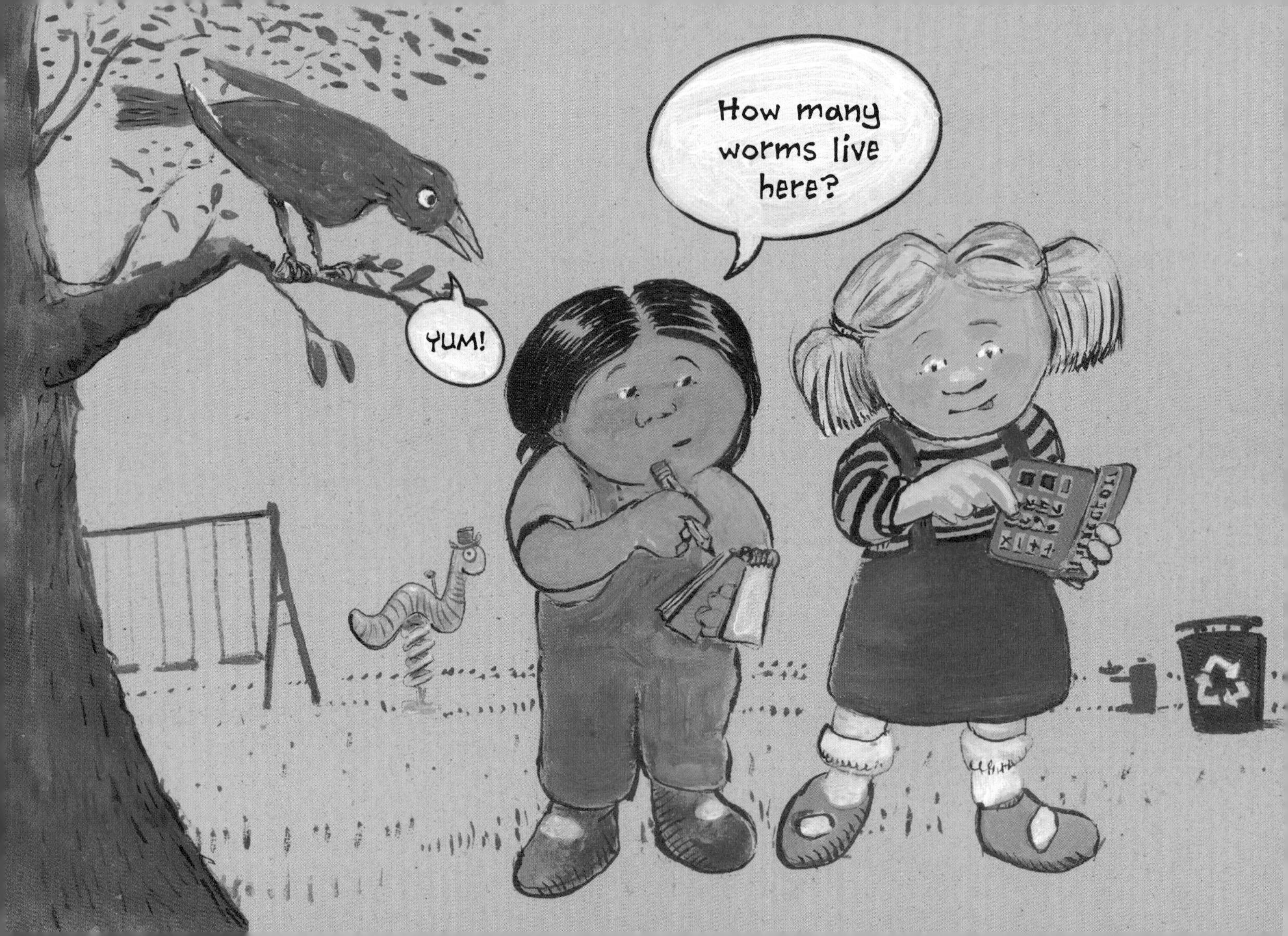
YUM!
How many worms live here?

Millions!
Millions!
Millions!
Millions!
Millions!
Millions!
Millions!
Millions!

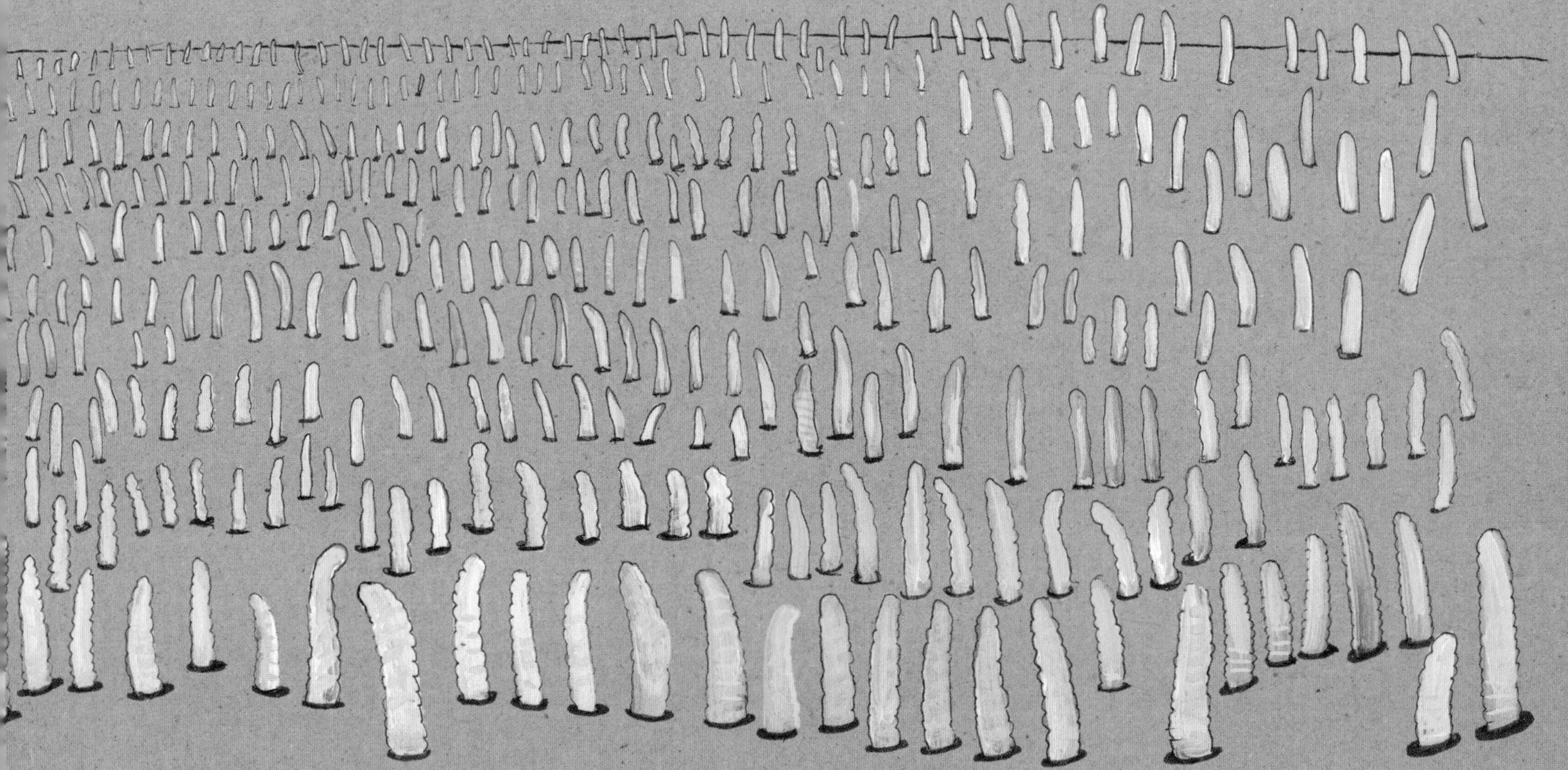

Over ONE MILLION worms can live in a small park.

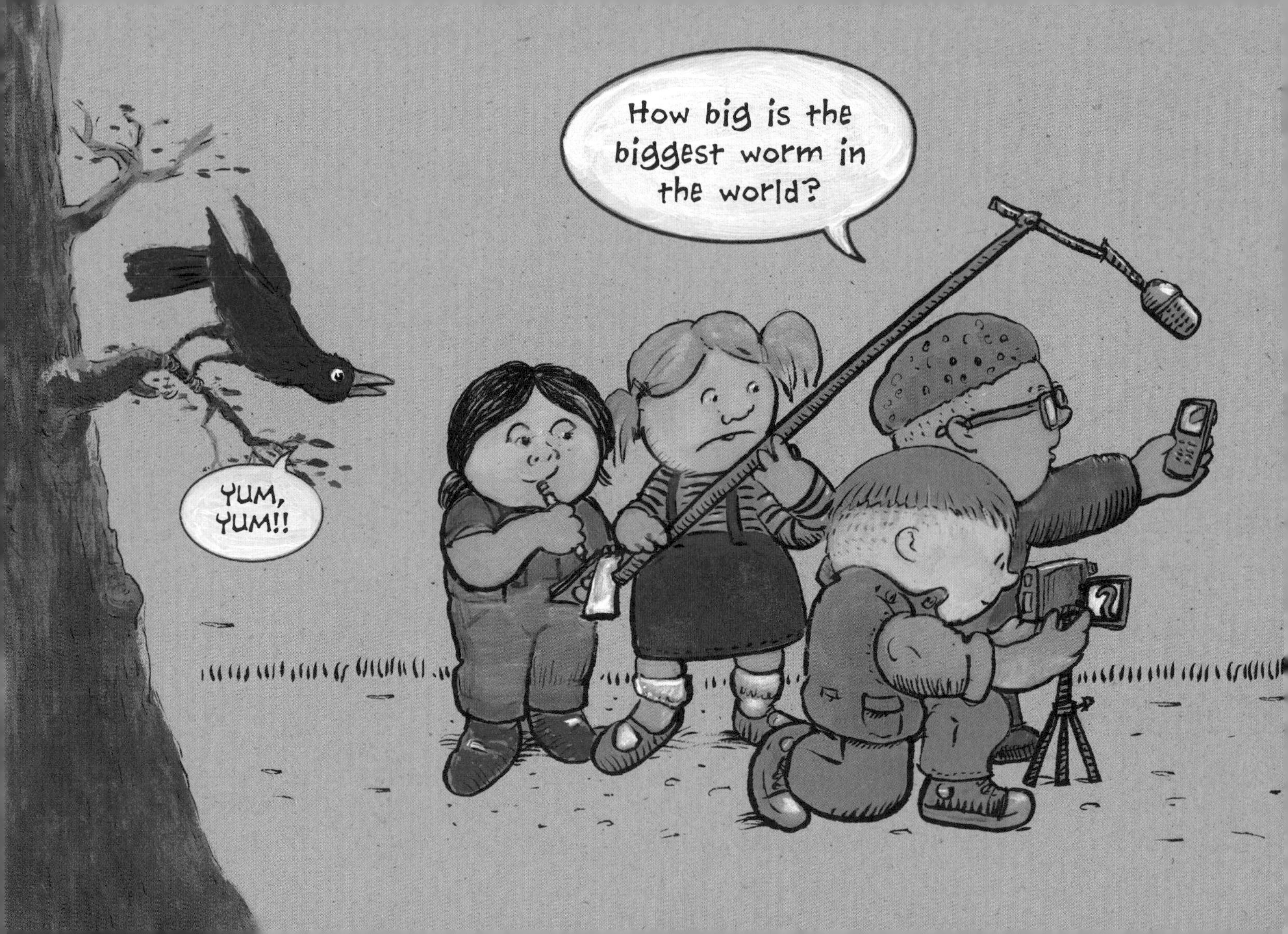
How big is the biggest worm in the world?
YUM, YUM!!

THE AUSTRALIAN GIPPSLAND WORM GROWS TO 10 FEET LONG.

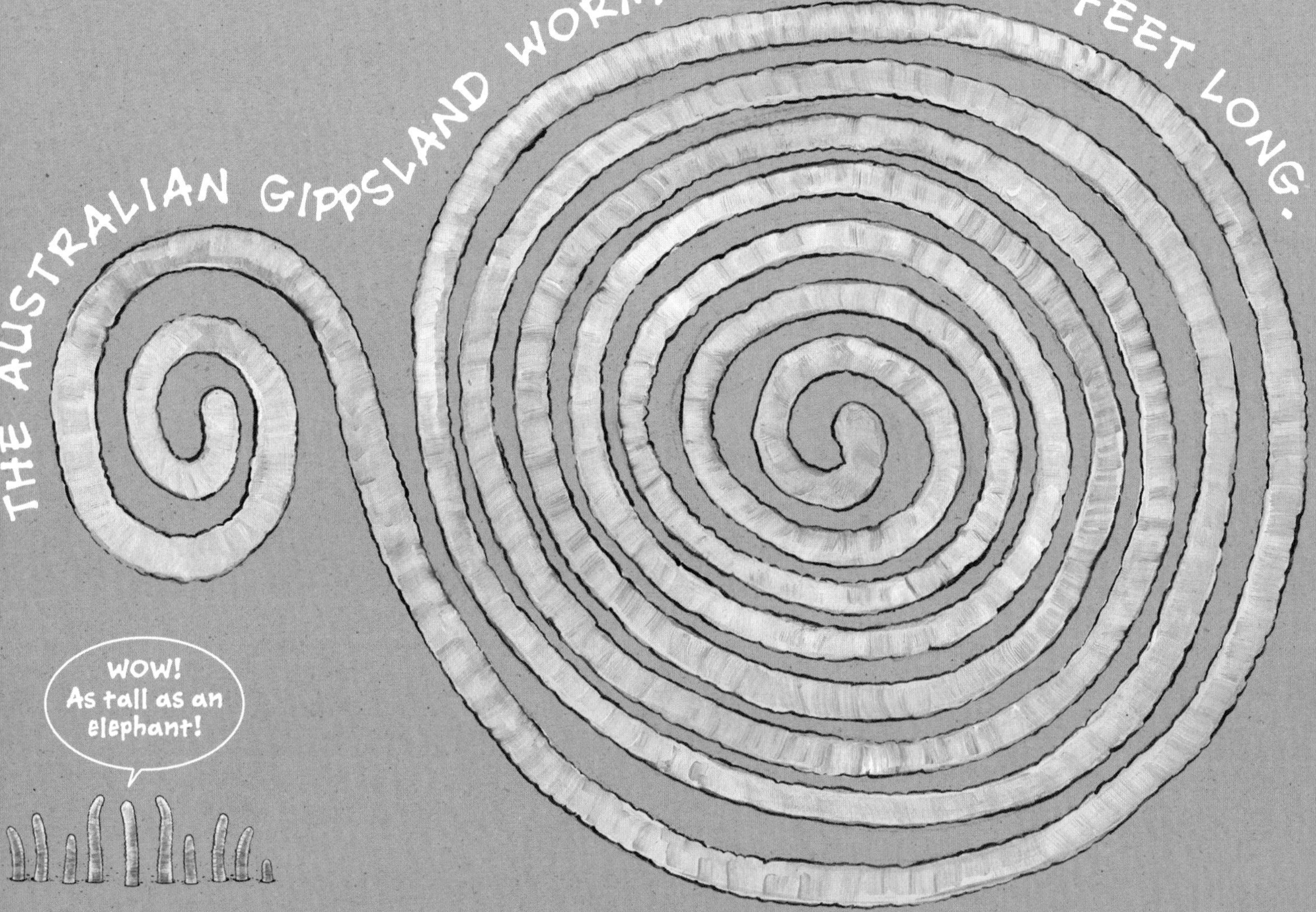
WOW!
As tall as an elephant!

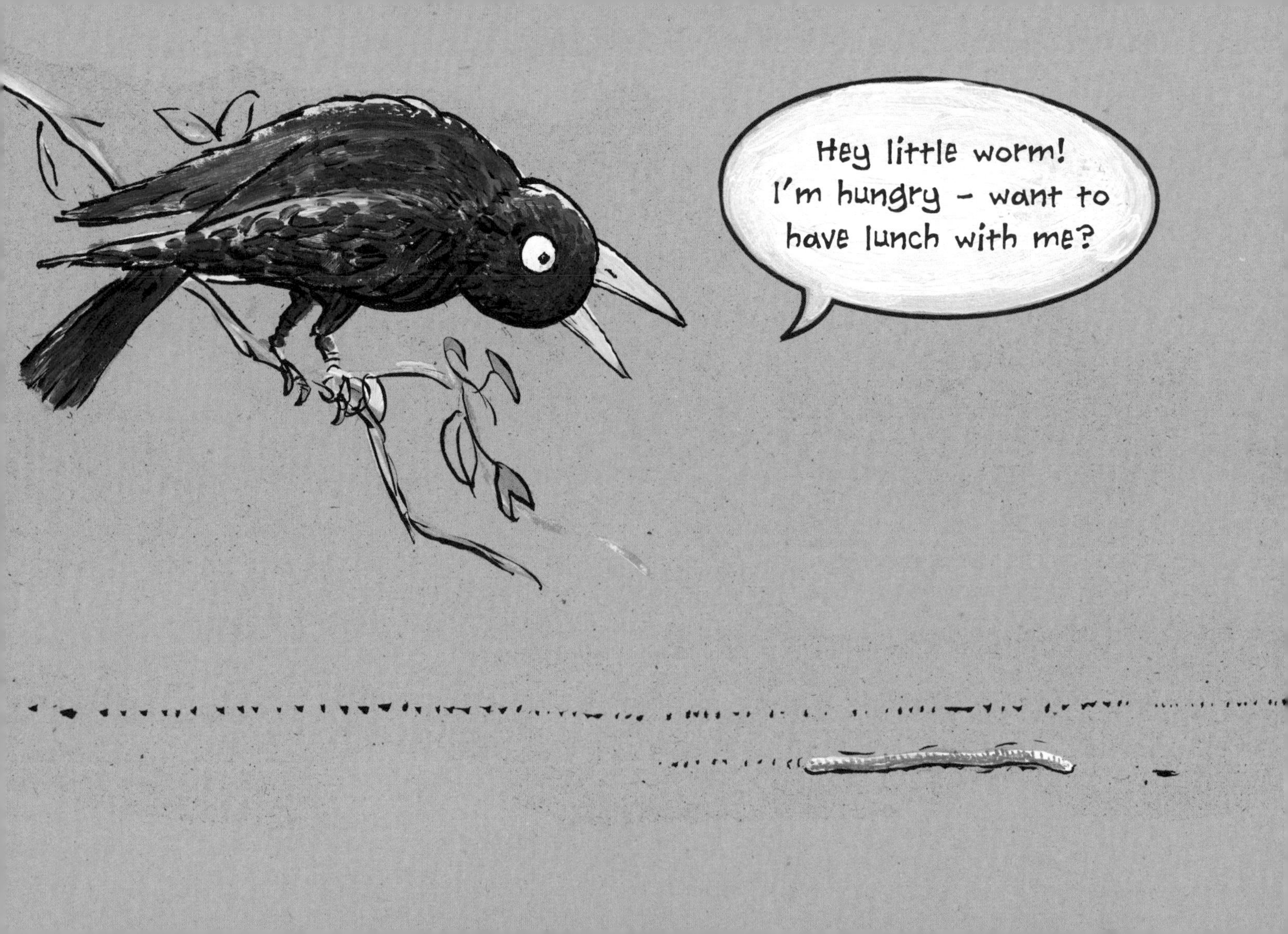
Hey little worm!
I'm hungry - want to
have lunch with me?

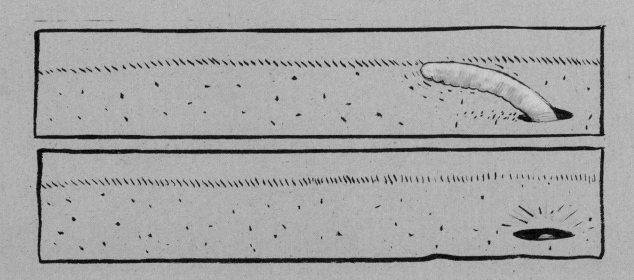

WHY DID THE LITTLE WORM GO AWAY?
WAS IT SOMETHING BLUEBIRD SAID?

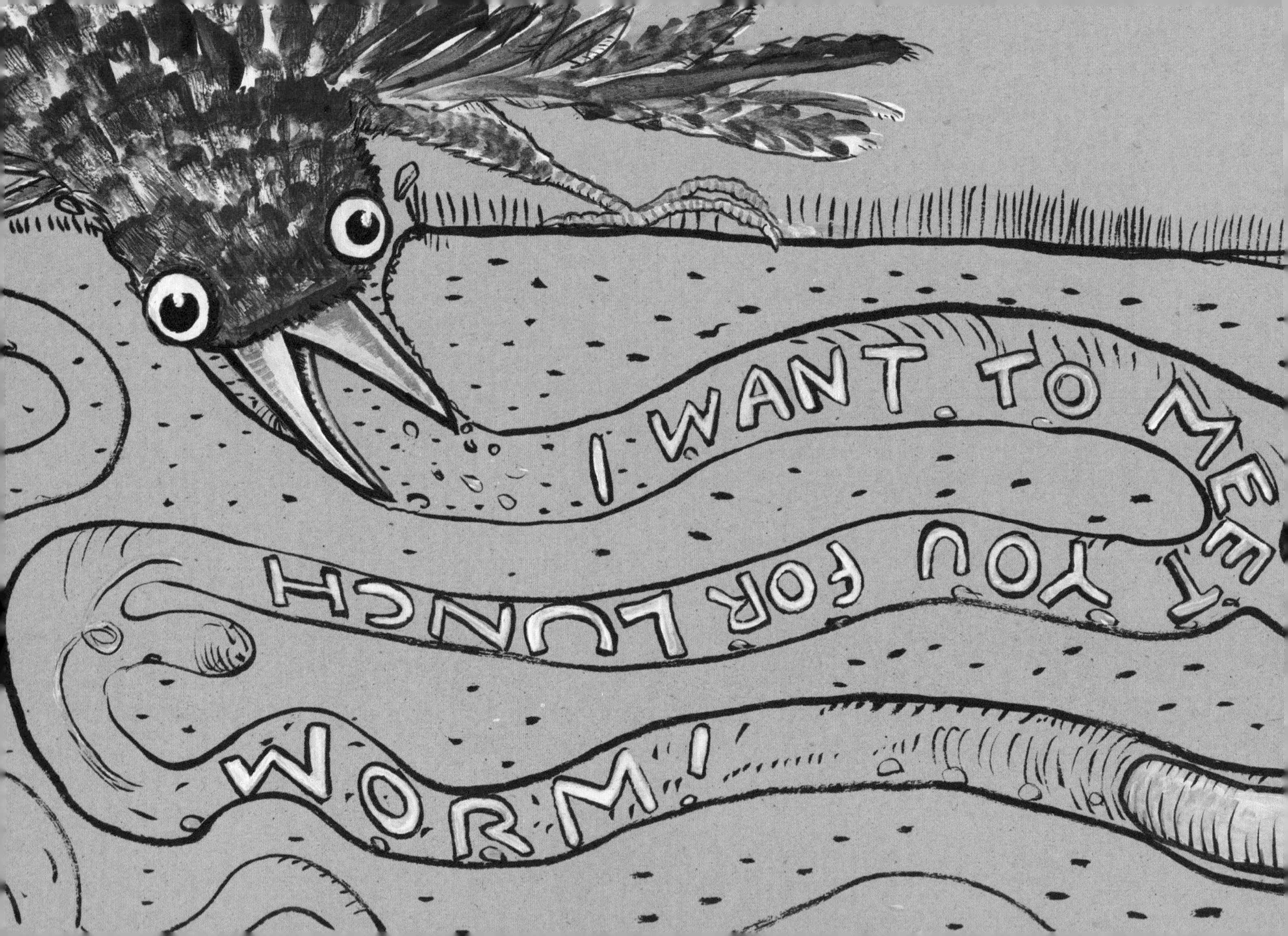
I WANT TO MEET YOU FOR LUNCH WORM!

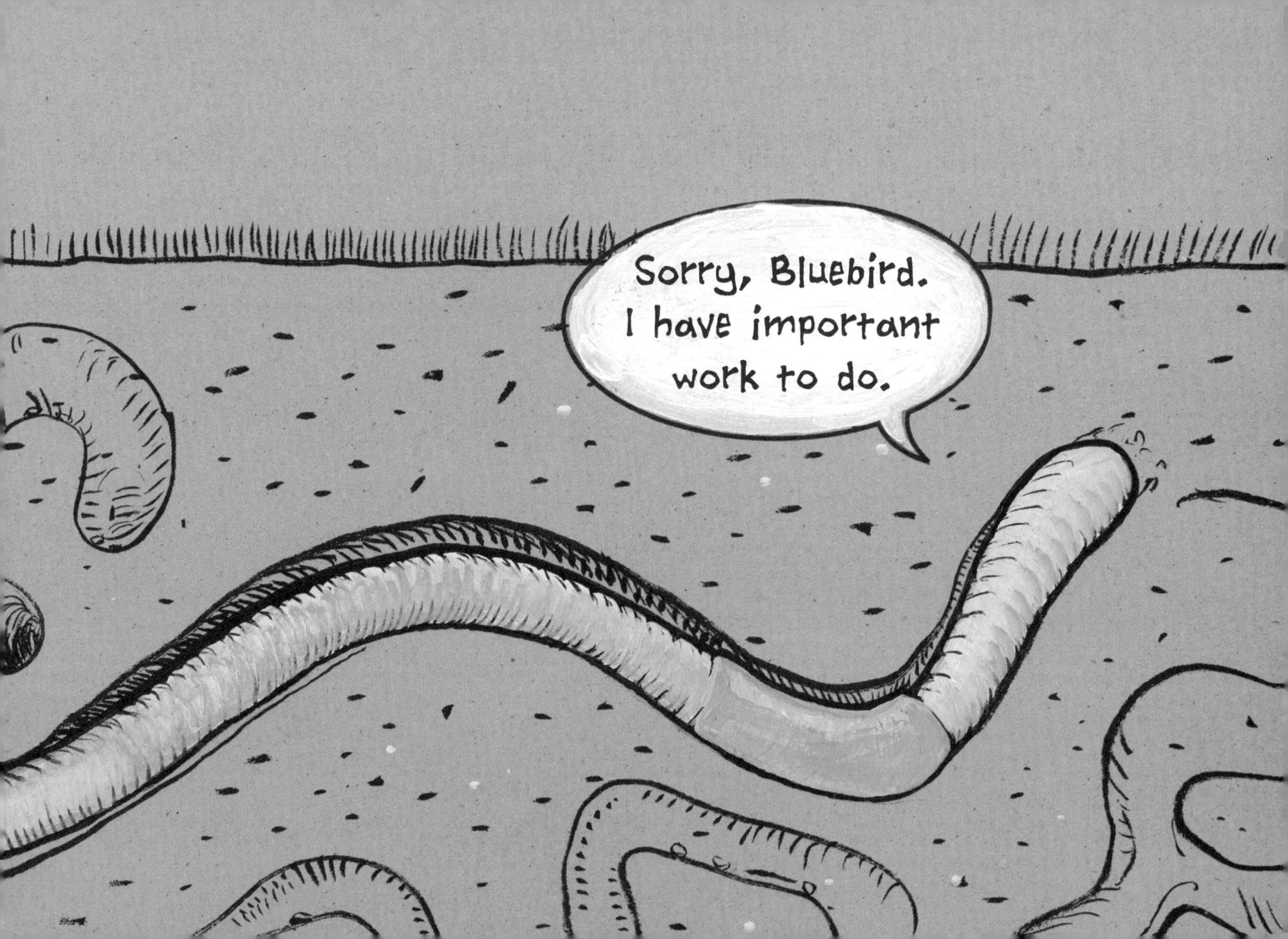
Sorry, Bluebird. I have important work to do.

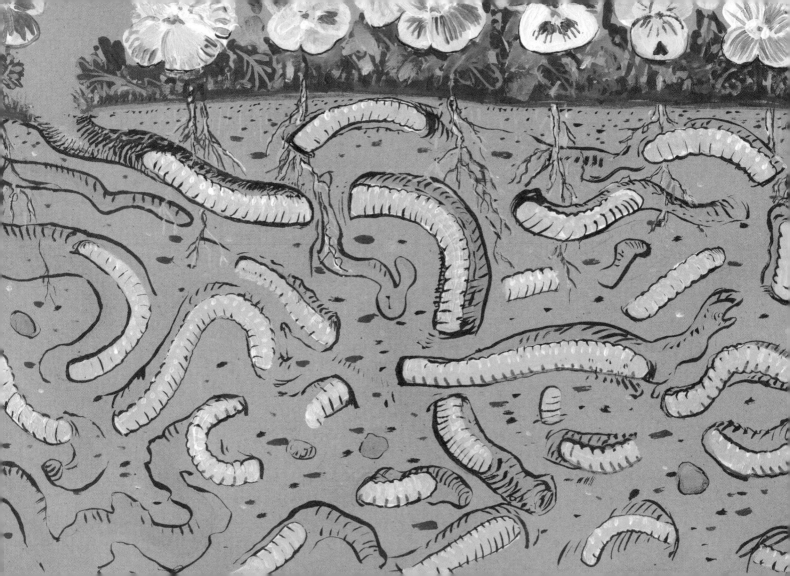

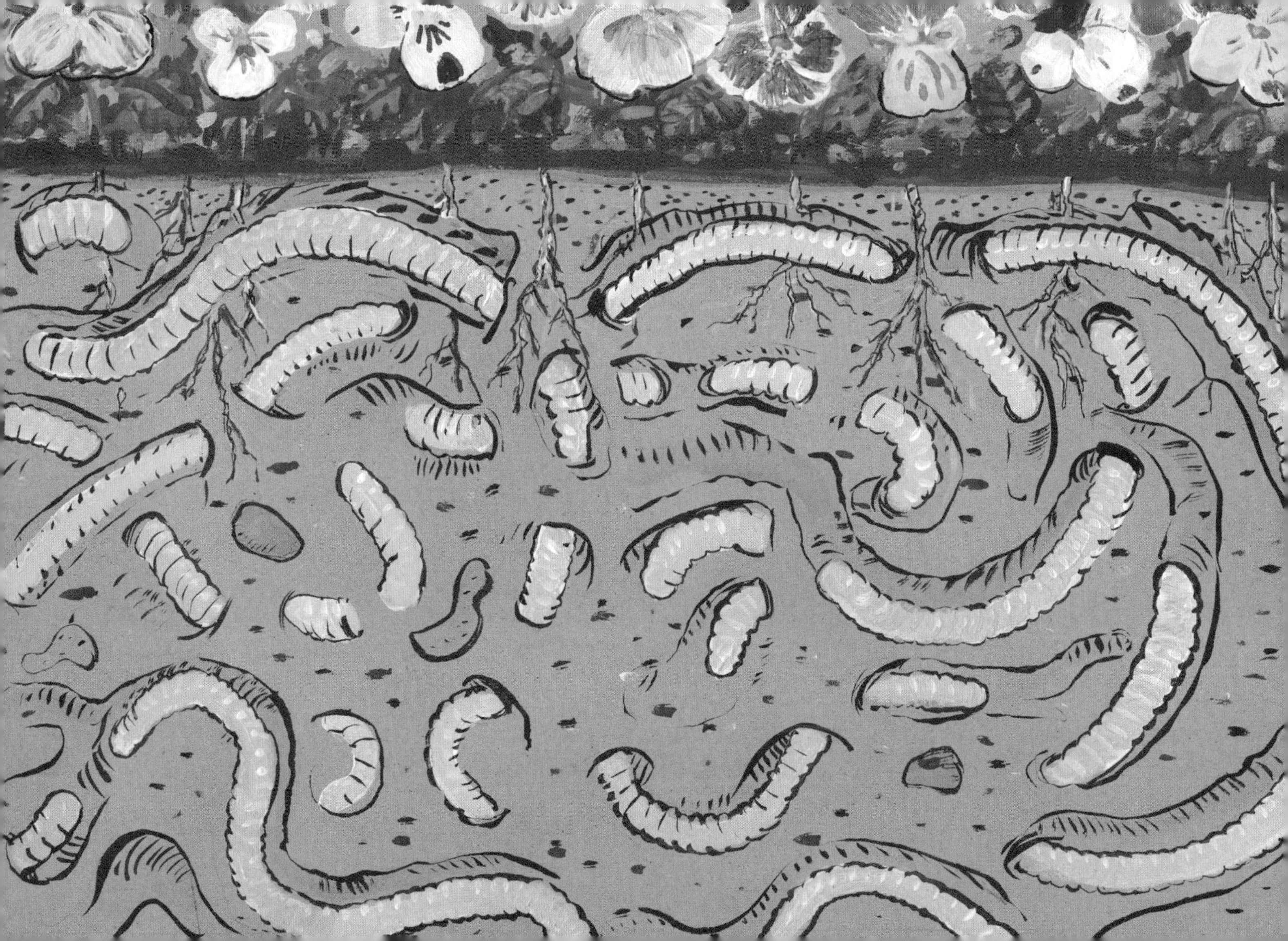

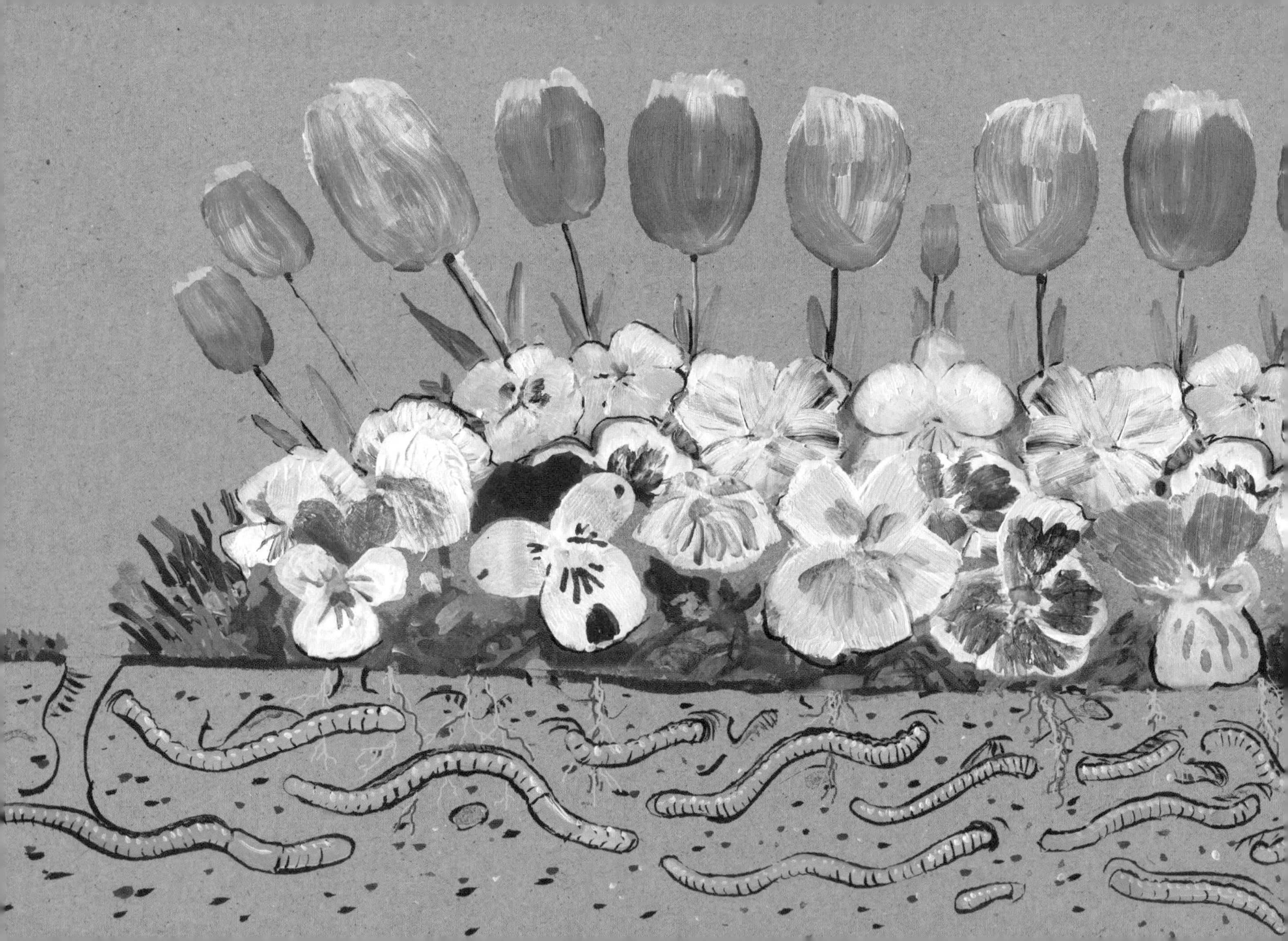

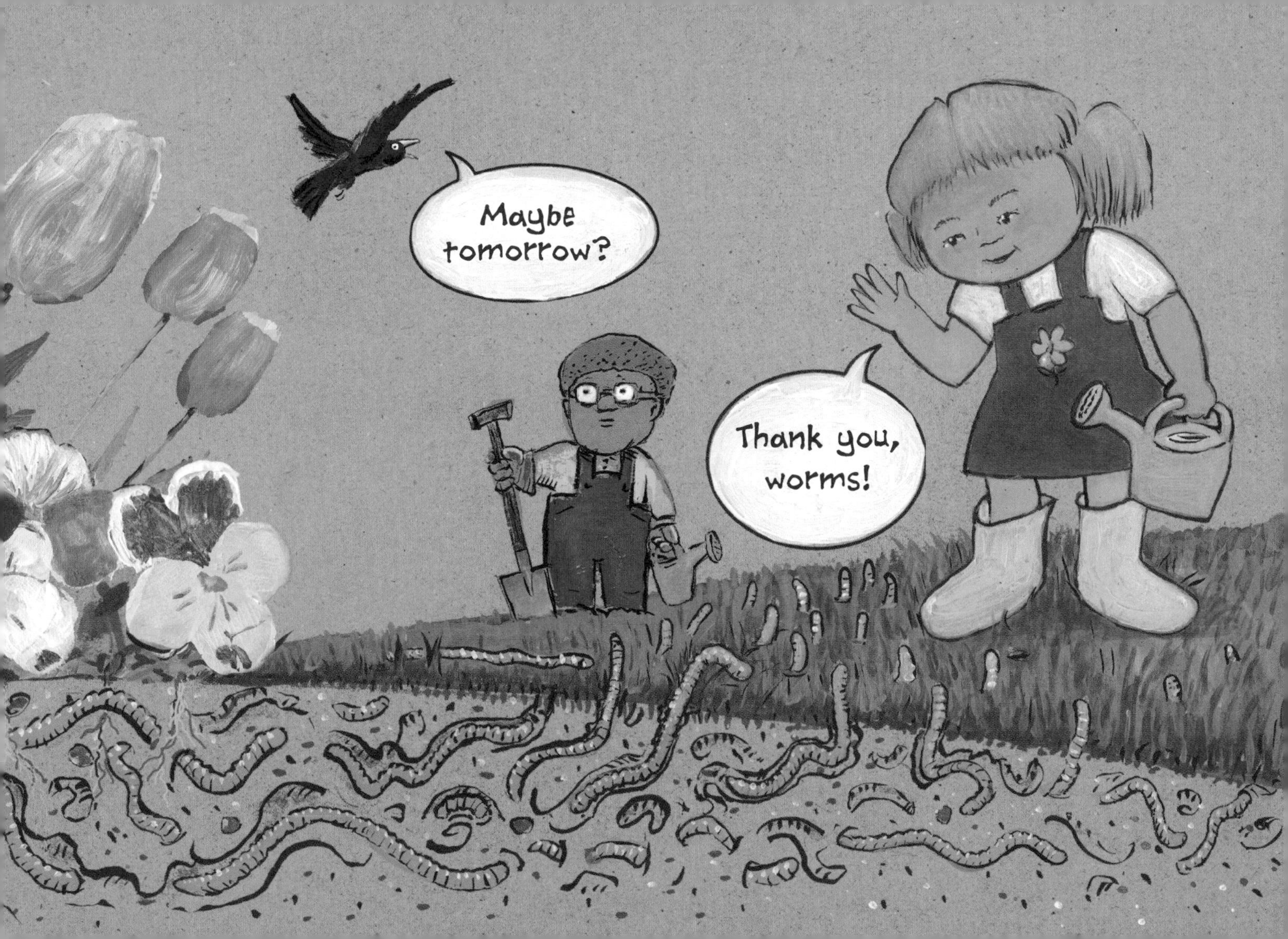
Maybe tomorrow?
Thank you, worms!

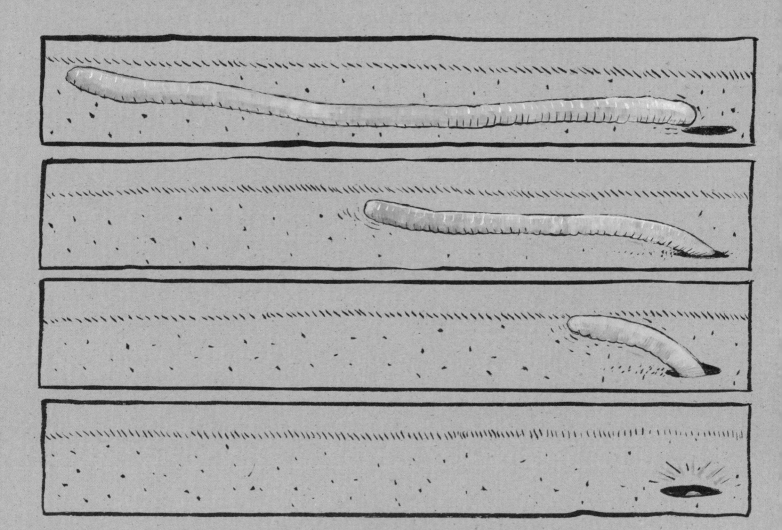

THE END

ABOUT THE AUTHOR

Kevin McCloskey teaches illustration at Kutztown University in Pennsylvania. He painted these worm pictures on recycled grocery bags because, just like worms, he believes in recycling.

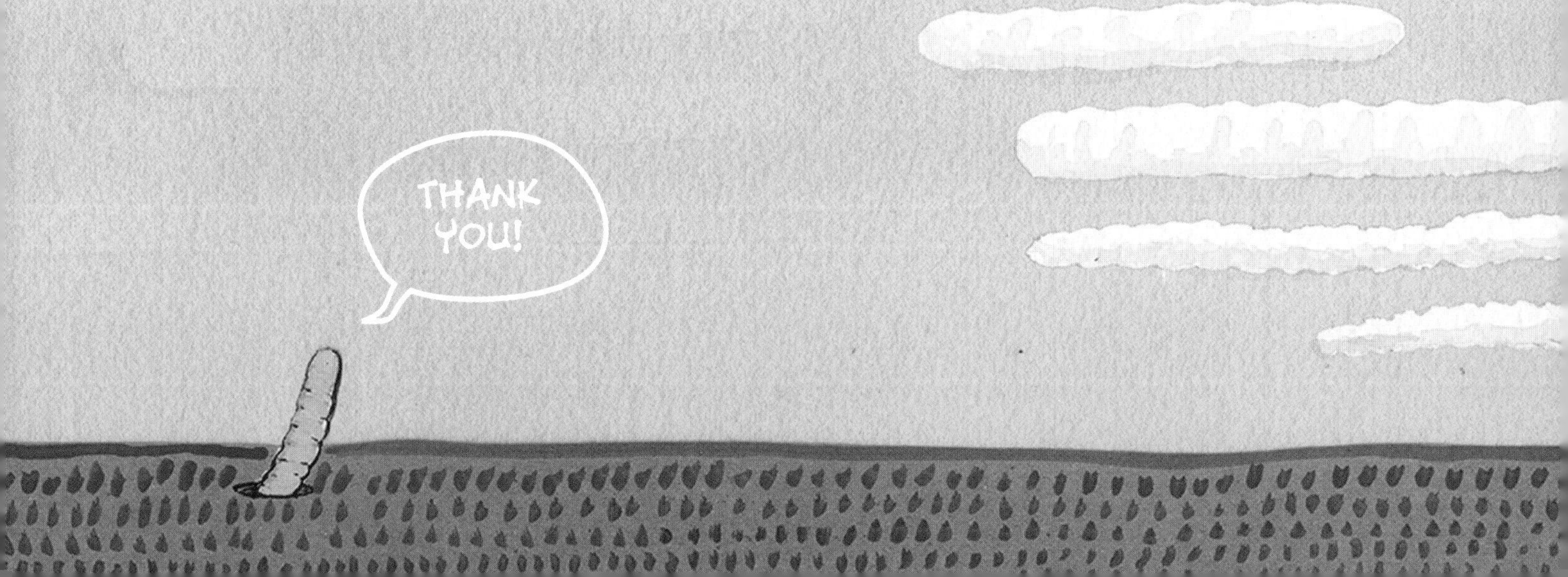
THANK YOU!

TIPS FOR PARENTS AND TEACHERS:

HOW TO READ COMICS WITH KIDS

Kids love comics! They are naturally drawn to the details in the pictures, which make them want to read the words. Comics beg for repeated readings and let both emerging and reluctant readers enjoy complex stories with a rich vocabulary. But since comics have their own grammar, here are a few tips for reading them with kids:

GUIDE YOUNG READERS: Use your finger to show your place in the text, but keep it at the bottom of the speaking character so it doesn't hide the very important facial expressions.

HAM IT UP! Think of the comic book story as a play and don't hesitate to read with expression and intonation. Assign parts or get kids to supply the sound effects, a great way to reinforce phonics skills.

LET THEM GUESS. Comics provide lots of context for the words, so emerging readers can make informed guesses. Like jigsaw puzzles, comics ask readers to make connections, so check a young audience's understanding by asking "What's this character thinking?" (but don't be surprised if a kid finds some of the comics' subtle details faster than you).

TALK ABOUT THE PICTURES. Point out how the artist paces the story with pauses (silent panels) or speeded-up action (a burst of short panels). Discuss how the size and shape of the panels carry meaning.

ABOVE ALL, ENJOY! There is of course never one right way to read, so go for the shared pleasure. Once children make the story happen in their imagination, they have discovered the thrill of reading, and you won't be able to stop them. At that point, just go get them more books, and more comics.